Original title:
Aloe Vera Verses

Author: Lorenzo Barrett
ISBN HARDBACK: 978-1-80581-788-8
ISBN PAPERBACK: 978-1-80581-315-6
ISBN EBOOK: 978-1-80581-788-8

The Healing Touch

A plant so green with a soothing flair,
It loves the sun and the humid air.
When you get burned or feel a sting,
This leafy gem sure makes you sing.

With sticky gel that cools your skin,
Rub it on good, let the fun begin!
If you forget, it won't hold a grudge,
But might just giggle, give you a nudge.

Where Prickles Meet Peace

Among the spines, there lies a treasure,
A calming balm, it brings us pleasure.
Though it looks fierce, don’t be misled,
This cactus friend’s all about spreadin' zen.

In sunny pots, they like to chill,
Sharing their joy with a wink and thrill.
Prickles on edges, soft hearts within,
Makes my heart dance, and let the laughs begin!

The Nature of Nurture

In nature’s grasp, they grow with pride,
Bending gently, like a joyful ride.
A gentle touch brings forth the glow,
While sipping sunshine, they put on a show.

Water them well, but don’t go wild,
Give them a drink, just like a child.
Their humor’s sharp, their smiles so wide,
In the world of greens, they’re the fun guide!

Anatomy of Freshness

In the land of gel and slippery slips,
Funky leaves dance with jiggly quips.
With every squeeze, laughter flows,
Who knew skincare could be so prose?

Turn that frown, give it a smirk,
This little guy loves to go berserk.
Nature's joker, green and spry,
With one funny glance, it’ll catch your eye!

Cactus Dreams and Drenched Blessings

In a pot on my sill, a prickly friend,
Wishing for water, a dry trend to end.
I told him to grin, he'd stay quite alive,
With dreams of the rain, he’d learn to thrive.

His spines stand tall, like a green little knight,
Guarding my secrets through long summer nights.
We laugh at the world, oh, what a great team,
In a sunbeam of hopes, we both chase a dream.

Soothe the Flame

When fireflies dance in the glow of the day,
My succulent giggles, it cheers up the gray.
I whisper to him, 'Do you feel the rush?'
He nods with a grin, saying, 'Hurry, don't shush!'

With laughter, we bask in the warmth of the sun,
Cooling the heat, we’ll have so much fun.
'This life’s quite a ride,' he seems to declare,
'With spines and with charm, I’ll always be there!'

Thorns That Comfort

Beneath all my prickles, a heart beats so true,
Each thorn tells a story, a giggle or two.
With quirks and odd shapes, we dance through the day,
Who knew furniture could have such fun play?

My prickly companion, he patches my soul,
Through ups and downs, he stays in control.
One day we'll conquer the wild ways of fate,
Together we laugh, while the world just waits.

A Quench for the Soul

In a world full of woe, I'm an herbalist’s muse,
With laughter and leaves, I shine, never lose.
Sipping sweet sunshine from dew on my leaf,
I curl up in joy, it’s beyond all belief.

What’s better than greens that dance in the light?
They tickle my spirit, oh what a delight!
With a wink and a smile, I invite you to share,
This joyful green potion, no worries or care.

Beneath the Skin

In the garden, green and bright,
Lies a plant, a wondrous sight.
With spiky leaves and gel within,
It laughs at woes—it’s where we begin.

Your sunburns feel that funny sting,
But this dear leaf could save a thing.
Just slice it up, the gel will shine,
Saying, "Don't worry! You’ll be fine!"

Remedy Near at Hand

Feeling clumsy, just my luck,
In comes the plant, a magic pluck.
Squeeze it out, a gooey blast,
Makes your fumbles fade so fast.

From kitchen burns to little scrapes,
This leaf's the hero that reshapes.
With every dollop, woes will ban,
It giggles softly, 'I'm your fan!'

Serenity in Succulence

In a pot, all poised and sleek,
This greensome friend can really speak.
With every squirt, it sings a tune,
Beneath the sun or sneaky moon.

Who knew this plant could bring such cheer?
A slice for fun, a drop for fear.
It winks and says, 'Your pain's just light,'
'With me around, it's all alright!'

Fluid Grace

Oh, the grace of this green delight,
With slippery swag, it takes flight.
On your skin, it dances free,
A jiggly joke, a gel-like spree.

Put it on, and soon you'll see,
Bumps and bruises laughing with glee.
Who knew that plants could play so fair?
Rubbing in joy, without a care!

Shelter from the Storm

In the corner, green and sly,
A plant that waves a polite hi.
When the rain falls thick and sly,
It chuckles, ‘No need to cry!’

With spiky arms, it stands so proud,
As thunder roars and lightning’s loud.
‘Come under my leaves,’ it seems to say,
‘Here, you’ll be safe, come what may!’

Nature’s Gentle Hand

A little gel that's calm and cool,
It’s the hero of a sunny school.
With a wink, it says, ‘Don’t you fret,
I’ve got your back, you can bet!’

When life gets messy, what a scene,
It slathers on like a friendly green.
A tickle and a giggle ensue,
‘You’ll laugh again, yes, it’s true!’

Verses of Vitality

Rub it here, rub it there,
Suddenly you've got flair!
Bumps and bruises whirl away,
With a grin, it likes to play.

Put it on, and dance with glee,
You'll feel as spry as can be.
For every cut and every burn,
This silly plant will take a turn!

The Desert’s Embrace

In the desert, standing tall,
Looking like it owns it all.
With a smile that's never grim,
It flings a hug, on a whim!

“Sandy feet? Come find your bliss!
With me, you can’t miss!”
It waves its arms, a funky dance,
“Let’s hydrate—give me a chance!”

Touch of the Earth’s Embrace

In a pot so green and bright,
Dancing under the sunlight,
I found a plant with spiky grace,
Bouncing back in every place.

With gel so cool, it's quite a treat,
For sunburns there's no better seat,
When life's a pinch or even worse,
My green friend cures it, ain't that a curse?

Nature's Gentle Muse

Oh, succulent with so much flair,
You watch me trip, you see, you stare,
I laugh as I reach out to embrace,
You poke me back, it’s quite the case!

In gardens lush, you sway with ease,
Making all the neighbors sneeze,
You charm them with your prickly ways,
Oh, how you brighten up our days!

Guardian of the Sun

Standing tall, you’re full of cheer,
Protecting me from all the fear,
Each sunny day a true delight,
You stand guard till the night’s twilight.

With your juice, I spread the fun,
Slipped on the floor, oh what a run!
You giggle back, it’s not a joke,
Together we will make the folks croak!

The Aloe Diaries

Dear diary, let’s have a chat,
Today I wore a green spiky hat,
As friends came by, I did a dance,
But tripped and fell, oh what a chance!

They laughed and rolled, what a scene,
A plant that tumbles, oh so keen,
Yet here I am, all healed and proud,
Aloe's charm, I shout it loud!

Green Tales of Restoration

In the garden, they claim it's a miracle,
A plant so green, it might just be mythical.
With leaves like a sword, brave and tall,
It stands alone, a hero to all.

I gave it some water, just a small cup,
But it grew like a monster, ready to erupt.
It winked at the cactus, with spines all around,
And laughed like a jester, proud of its crown.

A friend once said, "It’s a magic show!"
With goo that can heal, and who knows what flow?
I tried to use some on a silly old cut,
And ended up slippery—now I'm in a rut!

So here's to the plant, with skin made of gel,
It makes all of us laugh, and that's just swell.
Call it a remedy or a plant full of sass,
In the kingdom of greens, it's first in the class.

The Embrace of Nature

There once was a plant, its humor so bright,
It tickled the sun, made the shadows take flight.
With a squish and a splash, it danced with delight,
And showed all the weeds how to party all night.

“Oh my!” said the flower, “What’s that on your leaf?”
“Just my gel, darling, don’t you dare be so brief!
I’m here for the laughs, not the solemn old care,
Let’s glue this place together, without any flare!”

In a world full of frowns, it sprouted a grin,
“Just rub me on rash, I’ll make your skin thin!”
Everybody gathered, quite curious they peeked,
To see the plant making the garden so sleek.

So here’s to the laughs, from this green leafy doll,
It keeps us all giggling, it stands proud and tall.
With a touch of its magic, the fun will impart,
Nature’s own jester, with a healing heart.

Threads of Renewal

In a pot sits a spiky friend,
With a grin that won't end.
When I'm burned in the sun,
She whispers, "Honey, you've won!"

Her juice, a slippery delight,
Turns my woes into flight.
Slather it on like a cake,
And watch all the troubles quake!

Rhythms of Relief

In the fridge, a cool surprise,
Green magic promises the skies.
Rub it in and feel the cheer,
Who needs ice packs? Not here!

When my skin feels like toast,
I praise her like a ghost.
"Thank you, plant, you're quite the star,
You heal my skin like a bizarre!"

The Green Enchantment

In a garden, green and bold,
Her secrets wait to be told.
“Don’t bite me!” she seems to scream,
Yet in her, I see a dream!

With her spiky, sassy grin,
I feel the healing begin.
Sprinkle on some good ol' fun,
Who knew plants could be this won?!

Timeless Touch

In a world of creams and goos,
She's the one I always choose.
A squish, a squeeze, what a blast,
Time flies by when you're aghast!

Every day is like a show,
With my green gal in tow.
Her wisdom makes me feel alright,
Aloe, you're my go-to knight!

Song of Softness

In a garden where plants giggle,
Soft leaves dance, it's quite a wiggle.
When you scrape your knee in play,
This green buddy saves the day!

Stick it on like a second skin,
Turns out fun is where you begin.
With a smile and a cheeky grin,
Nature's helper, let the games spin!

A Sip of Nature’s Care

Pour me a cup of that green delight,
Sipping it slowly, oh what a sight!
A glug, a splash, it’s all in the fun,
Who knew a plant could be so pun?

With a twist and a turn, it's quite the treat,
Jelly-like goodness, that can’t be beat.
When life gets sticky, here's the flair,
Just a sip of nature, show you care!

The Green Comforter

Wrapped in softness, what a fine plight,
Skin is happy, the future looks bright.
In a world that might bring dull despair,
This green comforter always beware!

A dab here, a dab there, quite the mix,
Wobbly with joy, it plays its tricks.
Like a hug from Mother Nature herself,
Always ready, it's a true green elf!

Nature's Quiet Poem

Whispering leaves in the gentle breeze,
Composed of joy, they aim to please.
Each droplet of care, a soft-spoken shout,
Here's to the fun when in doubt!

A quirk of nature, here to bestow,
Making laughter as it grows slow.
In a world of chaos, it quietly blooms,
And brings forth joy, in all its rooms!

Embrace the Green

In the corner of my room, it stands tall,
A plant with spiky leaves, not at all small.
It drinks the sun and sips some rain,
Smile at its glory, and you'll forget the pain.

A wonder in a pot, so green and bright,
It can be a remedy, oh what a sight!
If it had a voice, it would surely say,
'Just rub me on your skin, it's the spa way!'

The Leafy Lullaby

Singing softly in the breeze, a tale so sweet,
Of how to soothe your skin with a simple treat.
A leaf so flexible, like a funny friend,
In jellified laughter, your worries will end.

It wiggles in the pot, a dance of delight,
With each little squeeze, it’s a future so bright.
Who knew that a plant could win life's little race?
A comedian in green with a cooling embrace!

Wisdom in the Wound

In every little scratch, it knows what to do,
Speaking secrets of healing, just like a guru.
Erasing those mishaps, like a magic wand,
Oh leafy magician, you're endlessly fond!

A drop on a scrape makes the pain go away,
In your plant-parent heart, it'll forever stay.
With jokes on its leaves, it whispers its plan,
'Just give me some sunshine and I'll be your fan!'

Healing Hues

Green and bright, the color of glee,
In jars and in drinks, oh me, oh my, see!
With a wink and a wave, it appears on the scene,
Turning frowns upside down like a jolly routine.

It's not just a plant; it's a party in green,
Sipping health boosts, like you're in a dream.
So gather your friends for a leafy high-five,
With humor and grace, the plant comes alive!

Nectar of the Desert

In a pot on the sill, it sits so proud,
A green little friend, drawing quite the crowd.
I poke at its leaves, they wiggle and shake,
It’s hiding some magic, make no mistake!

With a squirt and a squish, a gooey delight,
I sneak a small taste, oh what a weird bite!
It tastes like nothing, yet everything sweet,
This plant is a joker, can’t beat that feat!

Healing Ode to the Green Guardian

Oh, you wonderful thing with your spiky embrace,
You slide into tweaks with such adorable grace.
With a snip and a squeeze, you're ready to mend,
Who knew a green cactus could be such a friend?

When life gives you burns or a scratch in the night,
Call up your buddy, it'll make it all right.
With soothing-aid gel, it's a patch-up parade,
I swear you're a wizard, you've got it made!

The Succulent Silence

In the corner it sulks, quiet as a mouse,
Don’t let its calm look fool you, what a rouse!
When guests walk by, it rolls its green eyes,
Thinking, ‘Can’t they see I’m the best of the guys?’

It listens to gossip, but never tells tales,
With a smirk on its face, it never fails.
It thrives on neglect, what a peculiar quest,
A low-maintenance buddy, it’s truly the best!

Embracing the Leaf

Cuddling my plant is the best part of the day,
It doesn't complain, just knows how to sway.
With arms open wide, it embraces the sun,
Telling me stories of nature and fun.

Its leaves nod along while I dance in my room,
This plant's my sidekick, in laughter we bloom.
A friendship so green, totally surreal,
Together we giggle, sharing the feel!

Green Elixir of Life

In the garden, green and bright,
A plant that dances in sunlight.
With a nod and a wink, it thrives,
Chasing away our daily jives.

With sticky charm and healing flair,
It spruces up a troubled hair.
When life throws you a slice of strife,
Just grab a leaf, it cuts like a knife.

From cooking blunders to sunburned skin,
This leafy friend just grins and spins.
Mix it in a potion, just a dash,
You'll be laughing with every splash!

So keep it near, your green delight,
A source of giggles, day and night.
In nature's dance, it's quite the star,
Who knew such fun could grow this far?

Leaves of Soothing Secrets

Secrets wrapped in jagged leaves,
Promising more than one believes.
A calming jar in anyone's sight,
With splendid charms that feel just right.

Slap it on when life's a mess,
Turning frowns into happiness.
With a funny face, it beams up high,
'Just call on me when you're feeling shy!'

Mix it with yogurt, splash or spread,
Turn a dull meal to a party instead.
What wizardry is hidden deep,
In this plant that makes you leap?

So gather round, come take a peek,
This leafy friend has lots to tweak.
With a laugh and a bit of cheer,
You'll find delightful magic here!

Whispering Succulent Soliloquies

In sunny spots, they gather round,
Whispers soft, a funny sound.
'What tale do we tell today?'
The succulent giggles in its own way.

With soft green fingers, they poke and prod,
In their company, life feels like a nod.
'Rub my leaves, feel the cool,`
'Watch out for those who try to steal this jewel!'

They chat about last summer's sun,
And laugh at all the silly fun.
Growing stout with stories untold,
Each leaf a laugh, each stem pure gold.

So sit a while, let secrets unfurl,
With these garden pals, let laughter whirl.
For in their silence, wisdom sings,
And our funny hearts, to happiness, clings!

The Gel Within

Oh, the gel inside, a slick surprise,
It sparkles bright, a joy for eyes.
Catch it quick, and watch it flow,
A slippery friend, putting on a show.

In a fumble, it's there to save,
A soothing balm when you misbehave.
'Turn that burn into a gleeful cheer,
For I'm the gel you want right here!'

When life gets tough, and the sun burns hot,
This jiggly hero ties up the knot.
With a chuckle, it slips from hand to earth,
Bring on the humor, it's time for mirth!

So grab a spoon, and don't be shy,
This gel's for fun, just give it a try.
With every dollop, let laughter in,
For the joy of life is where we begin!

The Green Whisper

In the garden, there’s a chat,
A plant that’s sassy, not a brat.
With gel so slick and leaves so spry,
It knows the secrets, oh my, oh my!

It wiggles in the summer breeze,
Tickling toes and pinching knees.
One whiff of its herbal charm,
You’ll chuckle, but it means no harm!

When you’re sunburned, it takes the lead,
With soothing gel, it’s quite the breed!
Just don’t let it know it’s a plant,
Or it might start doing a funny dance!

So here's to the green and quirky sage,
With a sense of humor, it’s all the rage!
In the world of flora, it’s the star,
Throw a party, there’s fun to spar!

Sun-Kissed Clarity

In a pot upon the sill, it grins,
With sunny vibes, where laughter begins.
It says, 'A sip of my juicy treats,
Will fix your woes and dancing feats!'

Wavy leaves like little arms,
Swaying gently, they work their charms.
“Burnt your nose? Just take a dab,
I’ll turn that frown into a fab!”

On a summer day, so wild and bright,
This cheeky plant is pure delight.
Sun-kissed laughter, it knows the way,
To keep the blues and aches at bay.

“Just rub me here, and rub me there,
I’m not just pretty, I’m debonair.
Bears a secret, oh so slick,
It’s nature’s best, do take your pick!”

Secrets of the Solace Leaf

A mysterious leaf on the bathroom shelf,
Whispers secrets of health and self.
With a wink and a nudge, it’s full of fun,
‘Ready for summer? Let’s go run!’

It giggles when you pour the cream,
Turning your skin into a dream.
“Got a cut? Don’t cry, just breathe,
Squeeze my gel, and you'll believe!”

It rolls its eyes at those who frown,
‘Cause I’m in charge, I wear the crown!
With every dab, I bring the cheer,
Let’s laugh away the drips of fear!

Here’s to the leaf with humor untold,
Turning mishaps into stories bold.
So give it a pat, it deserves a cheer,
For every giggle and joyful tear!

A Journey Through the Leaves

Come take a ride on this leafy train,
Where laughter echoes, and there's no pain.
With every tickle along the skin,
It says, 'Let the fun and healing begin!'

Bouncing through gardens tight and round,
You'll find this plant, giggling sounds abound.
"Oh dear friend, hold on real tight,
We're off to chase the summer light!"

It may look simple, just green and bright,
But it knows how to party all night.
Just a dollop here, a dollop there,
And suddenly, you've got flair to spare!

So dance on the leaves, don't forget to play,
In this funny world, we'll laugh all day.
With its carefree spirit, raise a toast,
To the silly plant we love the most!

Leaves of Solace

In a pot on my sill, they reside,
Green and plump, with nothing to hide.
They giggle and dance in the warm sunlight,
Whispering secrets that feel just right.

When my skin has a burn, they cheer,
"We got this, friend! No need to fear!"
They slide like ninjas, smooth and sly,
Turning frowns into laughter, oh my!

I tell them my woes, they listen with glee,
"Your drama is cute, but just wait and see!"
With a pinch of their magic, they mend and they make,
Turning sizzle to chuckles for everyone's sake.

So here's to the leaves, with their humor divine,
Silly little wonder, so graciously fine.
They'll smile through winter, through rain, through sun,
With them by my side, I always have fun!

Healing Horizons

The pantry’s stocked, there’s no need to pout,
A remedy here that blocks all the clout.
When life gets too spicy with a jalapeño bite,
These little green champs come make it feel right.

Cactus cousins envy their gooey fame,
They've got the skills, and they’re never lame.
A dab here, a dab there, pain fades like a ghost,
With a smile on my face, they’re the company I boast.

"Make haste, my friend, grab a slice of our kin!"
Laughing with joy as the healing begins.
They promise a journey, a stroll down the lane,
With a chuckle or two, they wash away pain.

They’re more than a plant; they’re a friend indeed,
With puns and good humor, they fulfill every need.
So let’s raise our glasses to these healing blokes,
For the laughter and comfort amidst all the jokes!

Sunlit Lines of Life

In sunlight they stretch, reaching for grace,
With laughter and joy, they take their place.
The world can be quirky, but they mix it right,
With each sunny smile, they brighten my night.

"Feeling a chill? Just come on near!"
They sing through the pains, banishing fear.
A tickle of humor, a wink and a grin,
Turns gripes into giggles; let the laughter begin.

With every mishap, they're right in the fray,
"Did you say 'burn'? We're on our way!"
Sliding and slipping, in a sticky embrace,
They brighten bad days, leaving no trace of disgrace.

So here's to the leaves with their comic finesse,
Sprinkling cheer like it's a party, no less.
They teach us the art, of a life full of glee,
In the sun's warm embrace, they will always be free!

The Soothing Bounty

In a garden so wild, they quietly bloom,
Sending out laughter, dispelling all gloom.
With sticky surprises, they're ready to play,
Turning aches into giggles, come what may.

They squeeze out the joy from their vibrant green skin,
With a squirt and a laugh, let the fun begin.
"Got a sunburned smile? Come over here quick!"
Patching up hurts with their humor so slick.

In my little mishaps, they stand by my side,
With a playful punch, they take me for a ride.
"Did you really fall? Just watch and prepare!"
As they stretch out their leaves, shedding laughter and care.

So let's give a cheer for this comical plant,
With humor and healing, so vibrant, they chant.
Every drop and each stroke is a tickle and tease,
Turning life into joy with the greatest of ease!

Oasis of Calm in a Chaotic World

In the middle of chaos, here I sit,
With a plant that thrives, just a little bit.
It doesn’t fuss, it doesn’t frown,
While all my socks are scattered around.

It drinks the sun like it’s a cocktail,
While I just hope my car won’t fail.
With spiky edges and a gentle wink,
It’s the only one that makes me think.

In a world turned upside down and loud,
It stays so cool, never too proud.
Oh, how I envy its calm green grace,
While I search for my missing shoelace.

A little pot of weird, yet wise,
In a world of chaos, it’s a prize.
With goofy leaves, it waves at me,
Let's grab a drink, just plant and me!

Fragile Strength of Verdant Vessels

With leaves like armor, soft yet tough,
It laughs at thorns and calls them bluff.
“Oh please,” it giggles in the breeze,
“Your worries don’t matter, just sip some tea.”

It's not just pretty, it’s got some flair,
Takes all my stress and turns it to air.
When all’s a mess and I scream and shout,
It’s the quiet bud that spins it about.

Wonder how it bends without a break,
While I can’t even roll off the lake!
It’s a little sap that knows the dance,
Reminding me to loosen my pants.

And in its pot, it plays so bold,
With stories of strength waiting to be told.
Oh, pot of green, you’ve shown me right,
To laugh at my worries, day and night!

Poetry Embedded in Petals

In the garden of giggles, blooms a tale,
With petals that whisper, "Don't let's fail."
Each leaf a lyric, each stem a line,
It's a plant that's got rhythm; it's just divine!

"Let's write a sonnet," it calls with cheer,
While I trip on grass, my greatest fear.
The pollen dances, a jiving song,
I'm just hoping my dance moves aren't wrong!

With laughter hidden in green and gold,
It keeps my troubles in stories untold.
Its humor is sharp, like a well-timed pun,
A partner in crime when there's no more sun.

Oh leafy poet, let's recite,
Our quirky verses till the night.
With each little quirk of its playful sprout,
Life's a grand joke; let's give a shout!

Secrets Held in Leafy Confessions

Underneath those spiky plans,
Are secrets noted in green strands.
It giggles softly, “I know the way,
To keep your drama far at bay.”

With roots that hold and leaves that sway,
It hears my troubles day by day.
“Try a face mask; it’s worth a shot,”
Makes me think of what I forgot.

Whispers in green, they tell me tales,
Of cushy beds and cookie trails.
“Don’t be sad; pat my leaves,” it sighs,
And wraps me in its leafy guise.

So here’s a toast to squishy friends,
Who hold my secrets as life bends.
With a little shove from a smiling sprout,
I laugh at life with a joyful shout!

In the Embrace of Nature’s Balm

In sunlight's glow, they seem to laugh,
With spiky hats, they flaunt their craft.
They soak up woes, in their green attire,
Wrestling with sunburn, they never tire.

Oh, slippery gel! A summer’s friend,
A dab will do, it’s hard to pretend.
They offer hugs, both cool and bold,
Nature's balm, in the heat they hold.

Their leaves like swords, yet oh so sweet,
A grand alliance, who can't be beat!
From kitchen counter to the bedside stand,
In every corner, they take a stand.

With cheeky winks, they tell their tales,
Of sun-kissed days and breezy gales.
Who knew with spikes, they’d be so wise?
Nature's comedians in a green disguise.

The Secret Life of Spiny Friends

In quiet corners, they plot a scheme,
With spiky coats, they live the dream.
A weekend party, just them and the sun,
Unraveling secrets, oh what fun!

They giggle as squishy bugs pass by,
With prickly laughter, they feel so spry.
They spread their arms in a leafy dance,
Making the bees do a curious prance.

Night falls softly, they gossip away,
While moonlight bathes them in silvery play.
"Did you hear what the cactus said?"
They roll with laughter, spines and all, well-fed!

Morning brings sunlight, the party fades,
Back to their posts, like well-laid shade.
But just wait till night, the fun resumes,
In the secret life of spiny blooms.

Nectar of Resilience

A hardy warrior in the garden fight,
With armor so tough, and a heart so light.
Through drought and sun, they take a stand,
Spinning tales in the desert sand.

Their nectar flows, a soothing balm,
In tiny sips, so sweet and calm.
They cheer on plants with tender hearts,
A quirky crew, playing their parts.

A delightful mix of funny and bold,
In pots and patches, they shimmer like gold.
With every squirt, they save the day,
A resilient friend in the plant ballet.

Let's raise a toast, with wrinkled leaves,
To those green pals who never grieve.
In laughter and joy, we bask and thrive,
Thanks to their presence, we come alive!

Lush Soliloquy of Aloe

In gardens lush, a story unfolds,
With spiky friends, brave and bold.
One little leaf, speaking to the sun,
"Watch out, world, here comes the fun!"

With winks and nudges, they share their glee,
Mixing humor in photosynthesis spree.
Whispers of warmth in breezy air,
Creating a ruckus, without a care.

"Rub a bit here, oh don't be shy!
Chasing sunburns and waving goodbye."
They chuckle and giggle, with leaves so bright,
In their green embrace, all feels just right.

From garden beds to window sills,
They offer laughter and a million thrills.
So here's to the leaves, both crisp and spry,
In nature's embrace, they'll never say die!

Green Serenade of the Succulent

In my garden, there she stands,
A leafy wonder with sticky hands.
She craves the sun, soaks up the light,
In her green dress, a curious sight.

People stop, they take a peek,
Is she a plant, or some freaky geek?
With needles sharp and a wink of glee,
She's the best friend you'll never see!

A sip from her, you'll dance around,
Though one too many? You'll hit the ground!
Green goo pouring, that's her game,
Oh what joy, and oh, what shame!

So here's to her, my prickly mate,
With each leaf twist, she brings the fate.
In the sun, she's on a spree,
My funny friend, you and me!

Elixirs of the Desert

In the desert, she makes her mark,
With her slick gel, she's a real spark.
Jars of magic, glistening bright,
Her potions work—what a delight!

"Drink up," I hear the cacti say,
As I smear the goo in a silly way.
I feel so fresh, like a sun-kissed peach,
While trying hard not to screech!

Patch up those scrapes, and cure that rash,
She said with a grin, ready to splash.
But oops! A slip! Now I'm a mess,
Goo on my face, oh what duress!

So laugh with me, at her grand show,
Bottled laughter, too much to stow.
In the desert, life's a tease,
Thanks to the plant that gives with ease!

Healing with Nature's Touch

Oh what fun, this healing spree,
Oozing gifts from a leaf so free.
Mix it up, with a dash of style,
Who knew nature could make us smile?

Got a burn? Here's the plan,
Rub it down, be a happy fan.
But careful now, don't overdo,
Or you'll be stuck in your own goo!

I thought I'd look like a movie star,
Instead, I'm a sticky green jar.
Who needs glam when you've got grace,
In a leafy hug, life finds its place!

With her touch, we laugh and tease,
Every mishap met with ease.
Nature's healer, what a bunch,
Healing hands, plus a funny crunch!

Whispers from the Leafy Healer

In the corner, she gives a wink,
With whispers soft, more than you think.
“Come closer, dear,” she gently hums,
I step near, feeling the drums!

“Better grab a scoop for your skin,”
She says with a grin, “Let the fun begin!”
Spreading slicks, like a bubbly cake,
Oh the trouble, oh the mistake!

“Dude, you’re a mess!” a friend exclaims,
As green goo flows like silly games.
But I just chuckle, in this sticky affair,
With my leafy buddy, we make quite the pair!

So join the laughter, embrace the cheer,
With each little scoop, the fun is clear.
Whispers of joy in each squishy touch,
Leafy healer, I love you so much!

Nature's Silk and Thorns

In the garden, a plant so grand,
With leaves that look like a green hand.
It softens skin with a gentle touch,
But watch those spikes; they don’t care much!

A potion of magic in every leaf,
If only my neighbor, it could relieve!
He tried to make tea, but oh, what a twist,
Now he just winks at plants he once kissed!

When summer hits and sun’s ablaze,
It thrives in heat, it loves those rays.
I tried to water it with lemonade,
Now it only sings, I’m afraid of shade!

So here's to the plant that won't give up,
With spiky smiles, it fills my cup.
A comical friend with charm and grace,
Witty green sage in nature's embrace.

Dewdrops of Resilience

In the dawn light, a shimmer and glow,
Droplets hang on leaves, putting on a show.
I tried to catch one; it slipped away,
Now my shirt's wet—what a clumsy display!

They say it’s good for burns and woes,
But not if you’re racing to beat your toes.
I made a face mask, thought it was bold,
Ended up looking like a moldy old troll!

The garden's wisdom spills with glee,
A healer’s treasure; so fun to see.
But here’s a warning for the festive glee,
Don’t dance around; it’s not a cup of tea!

With resilience strong, it makes us cheer,
This spiky friend brings love, oh dear!
A dewy delight with laughter entwined,
In this whacky world, true joy we find.

A Tapestry of Healing Green

In a corner where sunshine beams,
Lies a tapestry woven of playful dreams.
A leaf says, 'Hello!' with a sassy grin,
While the pot nearby just wants to win!

“Apply it here!” shouts out my friend,
But accidentally, she went for the blend.
Now her soup’s thick with a gelled surprise,
That’s not quite the soup of health that she cries!

Each leaf a patch in nature’s quilt,
Cures skin and burns and maybe some guilt.
But you best read the label, make sure to check,
Or the side effects could make you a wreck!

So on this wild botanical ride,
Embrace the quirks, let laughter reside.
In a world full of charm, let’s dance and spin,
With a healing green that makes the heart grin!

The Herbal Chronicles

Gather 'round for a tale of cheer,
Of herbal heroes who conquer fear.
A warrior plant with a spiky crown,
Using laughter, it won't let you down!

A potion brewed with winks and jest,
But one wrong move, and it's a quest.
I tried to mix it with garlic bread,
Now my dinner just wants to be fed!

Let's not forget the healing art,
Of leafy greens that play a part.
Like little comedians in the sun,
A chuckle a day keeps the doctor undone!

So here's to the roots of our quirky treat,
Plant friends that bring joy, so sweet.
With a hearty laugh and a little glee,
These herbal chronicles set us free!

The Gentle Resilience

In the corner, a plant so bright,
Waving hello to the morning light.
With a wink and a stretch, it stands so tall,
Who knew a leaf could have such a ball?

When it rains, it doesn’t pout,
Just drinks up the drops, and spins about.
A little warrior, soft yet bold,
Saving the world, or so I'm told!

With every scratch and every bruise,
It offers comfort, it’s never a snooze.
A healing touch, a soothing balm,
This little hero remains so calm!

So raise a glass, let's give a cheer,
To this green friend, oh so dear!
With laughter in every sticky crack,
It steals the scene, and that’s a fact!

Softness Beneath the Surface

With a look so cute, it steals the show,
A spiky beauty, soft as dough.
Givers of hugs, it plays it cool,
In the plant world, it’s nobody's fool!

Behind the spikes lies the gooey treat,
A slippery substance, oh so sweet!
In smoothies or salads, you can’t go wrong,
This leaf’s got talent; it’s singing a song!

When life gets tough and starts to scrape,
Just reach for this green, it’s pure escape.
A squishy squeeze and you’ll find your way,
Turning your blues into a sunny day!

So let’s celebrate the magic within,
That little plant with a cheeky grin.
A soft embrace in a prickly pack,
With all its might, it’ll never crack!

Echoes of the Earth

From ancient times, a tale unfolds,
Of green leaves whispering secrets untold.
Roots deep in the ground, they dance and sway,
With stories from the past that still play.

In a world of chaos, where plants have to brawl,
This one stands firm, never to fall.
With a laugh and a wink, it greets the sun,
"Bring on the battles! They'll be all in fun!"

In the garden, it's the jester, it seems,
Wearing a crown made of sunlight beams.
With every new sprout, it steals the scene,
The funniest friend, bright and green!

So join in the laughter, give a little cheer,
For this Earth's echo, forever sincere.
In the symphony of life, it plays its part,
With joy in its leaves, and love in its heart!

An Ode to Green Guardians

In the land of the quirky, it takes the stage,
Guarding the home with wisdom of age.
A trusty companion with no fear,
"Bumps and bruises? Bring 'em here!"

With a flick of its leaf and a tilt of its head,
It turns all the frowns back into bread.
"Got a problem? I'm your knight!
Just smother it with my gooey delight!"

In the wild wilderness of life's crazy fray,
This bright green guru knows how to play.
Chuckles and giggles from each little quirk,
Let's all take note, we've got work to work!

So here's to the guardians, strong and spry,
Waving and laughing as time goes by.
Leaves in the breeze, they dance and prance,
In this wild, wacky, glorious dance!

The Stillness of Healing Greens

In the garden, green and spry,
A plant stands tall, it won't cry.
Its leaves are thick, a comical sight,
Ready to help and to fight.

With a squeeze, it oozes out,
A gel that makes us shout!
"What sorcery is this?" we jest,
As we slather on, it's the best!

In every home, a loyal friend,
When skin goes wild, it will mend.
From sunburned snags to tiny cuts,
This leaf of green truly struts!

So here’s to plants, who quietly play,
With a smile that says, “I save the day!”
In stillness, they heal with no fuss,
While we laugh and make a big plus!

Layers of Green and Gold

A bold green leaf with edges sharp,
Under sunlight, it plays the harp.
Its layers hide a secret lore,
Of healing wonders, who could ask for more?

Each slice reveals a gooey thrill,
We chuckle as we pour and spill.
It's sticky and it's oh so grand,
A natural touch, from Mother's hand.

The skin can roar, it can moan,
But with this magic, it feels at home.
In pots and bowls, it sits quite sly,
"Don't forget me!" it seems to cry.

So next time skin puts on a show,
Grab that green friend, don't be slow!
For every tear and frown it mends,
With layers of joy, it never ends!

Nature's Healing Letters

In nature’s book, it writes in green,
A plant that’s more than it may seem.
With every scratch, a laugh, we share,
Our healer waits, it looks so rare.

It whispers tales of sun and soil,
Of every cut, and how to spoil.
We dab it here and smear it there,
In sticky fun, we do not care!

Like letters penned in leafy ink,
It teaches us to pause and think.
For in its presence, we all can see,
Healing's not just mystery!

So gather round and take a peek,
To nature’s letters, so unique.
With laughter bright, let’s celebrate,
This leafy hero, oh so great!

Prickly Wisdom

With prickly skin, it looks quite fierce,
A bit of caution, it does pierce.
But neither fear nor tear should reign,
For wisdom hides within that pain.

Squeeze it gently, don't be shy,
It's here to help, oh my, oh my!
A glee-filled potion just for us,
In this green hug, there's no fuss.

Though prickly friends may look unkind,
They've got compassion baked in their rind.
So laugh at quirks, with a wink or two,
For healing plants can be funny too!

Let's strike a pose with our green pals,
Embrace the quirks and giggle, y'all!
In every prick, a laugh we find,
With prickly wisdom, let's unwind!

Life’s Gentle Phytotherapy

In the garden, plants do sway,
One looks like it’s here to play,
With its green arms up in cheer,
Sipping sunshine, never fear.

Spotted leaf, soft and smooth,
Makes my skin dance and groove,
Whispers of magic in the air,
Moisture's friend, with dazzling flair.

“Eat me not!” it seems to jest,
Yet pleads for hugs, it’s truly blessed,
A simple friend with funny tricks,
In this green life, it surely clicks.

In the breeze, its laughter sings,
Turning frowns to happy things,
Nature’s joke in shades of green,
A healing hero, quite the scene!

Nature's Green First Aid

In the kitchen, what a sight,
A leafy gem, oh so bright,
Band-aids, crèmes, all on the shelf,
But this one tends to heal itself.

Cut a leaf, it starts to bleed,
The gooey gold is all I need,
For burns and blunders, it's my muse,
Jesters wear capes, I wear the ooze.

When I trip and take a fall,
I've got a remedy that's tall,
With a wink and a gelled embrace,
It turns my frown to a silly face.

Friends will laugh at my green stash,
Wondering if it's a treasure cache,
But I just grin and take a slice,
Nature's chuckle, oh so nice!

Embracing the Bitter and the Sweet

A prickly pal with a twisty grin,
Sassy in leaves, where to begin?
It offers nectar, yet warns me so,
With every touch, it's quite a show.

Crafty in nature, it plays the part,
Of beauty's potion with a cheeky heart,
Bitter and sweet in a whimsical dance,
One sip of its magic, puts me in a trance.

In salads or drinks, it steals the show,
But careful now, not too much flow,
It winks at me from the kitchen shelf,
“Use with care, or take the shelf!”

Sipping its secrets with a smile,
This leaf buddy has style and guile,
A comedy in gardens bright and neat,
A blend of life, oh, what a treat!

Tales of the Watered Leaf

In a pot, it spills a tale,
Wiggling leaves like a ship's sail,
Watered softly, it starts to dance,
Longing for sun, oh, what a chance!

It gathers stories from each droplet,
Sharing wisdom in a pocket,
Of how to stay cool in the sun,
And laugh at life, oh what fun!

When I am weary, I give a sigh,
"Leafy friend, help me comply!"
It chuckles softly and gives a tap,
With gentle care, it takes my nap.

So here's to tales from my green delight,
With every poke, it takes flight,
A sense of humor, a gentle jest,
In the garden, it's truly blessed!

Resilience Rooted in Earth

In the garden, a plant stands tall,
With leaves like swords, it won't fall.
In drought or flood, it laughs with glee,
A tough little dude, just like me!

It drinks up sunshine, sips some rain,
Flashes a grin, ignores the strain.
Roots deep and wide, oh what a sight,
This leafy warrior, ready to fight!

Neighbors may frown, some call it odd,
But this green friend, gives a big nod.
With every poke and prod it gleams,
A champion plant, living the dreams!

So here's to resilience, stretching so high,
Laughing at troubles as they pass by.
In the garden of life, it's truly the best,
This quirky green friend, who handles the rest!

Sips of Serenity from the Garden

In a pot by the window, a drink divine,
One sip of the juice, and all is fine.
A remedy brewed from nature's zest,
Even grandma claims it's better than rest!

With a wink and a giggle, I pour me a glass,
Say bye to my worries, let troubles just pass.
It's sticky and gooey, like a hand in the jam,
But one little taste, and I feel like a ham!

The garden whispers secrets, sweet and sincere,
"Drink up, my friend, you've naught to fear!"
A potion of calm, served tall or short,
Sipping with glee, I feel like a sport!

So let's raise a toast, to this fun little brew,
A sip of serenity, for me and for you.
In this world full of chaos, I take it with glee,
This quirky green liquid, setting my mind free!

Sun-Kissed Remedies

Under the sun, they bask and glow,
Tiny green soldiers in a bright row.
Every leaf a pillow, soft and bright,
A sun-kissed remedy, what a delight!

Mix up the magic, a potion in hand,
Glide through the garden, oh isn't it grand!
With a pinch of this, and a splash of that,
You'd think I'm a wizard in a tall, funny hat!

The neighbors all ponder, a curious sight,
"What's that you're brewing?" It's laughter and light!
A dab for the itch, a drop for the cough,
Using green magic, I finally scoff!

The sun shines brighter, and the smiles grow wide,
With every remedy, it's a joyful ride.
So here's to the leaves, the gifts from above,
In the garden of giggles, they shower us with love!

Beneath the Protective Skin

Beneath the layers, a treasure awaits,
An inner healer that just elevates.
With a peel and a poke, it gives a cheer,
"What's in my guts? Oh, have no fear!"

A squish and a squeeze, what fun it brings,
Slippery and silky, it's the joy of things.
Dab it, rub it, oh what a thrill,
Making my skin feel cool and quite chill!

A quirky concoction, straight from the core,
Each droplet giggles, leaving me wanting more.
With every use, I feel like a star,
No need for the doctor; I'll raise the bar!

So here's to the magic encased in green,
A playful protector, my beauty machine.
With laughter and joy, it stands in my bin,
A funny little healer, let the fun begin!

Elixirs of Essence

In the kitchen, a green jar stands,
With a potion that's made for happy hands.
It smooths out the skin and brightens the day,
But put it on toast? Oh, that's just great play!

A little dab here, a little dab there,
A remedy found, nobody can compare.
It’s sticky and gooey, like a kid's great art,
But makes you feel like a botanical heart.

Mix it with laughter, toss in some cheer,
Forget all your troubles, they won’t come near.
Like a friend who’s green, and oh so bright,
A little slice of joy in morning light.

So if you’re feeling a bit out of whack,
Just grab the green jar, don’t hold back.
In life’s grand buffet, it’s the weirdest treat,
A quirky delight, can’t be beat!

Nature's Gentle Arm

In the garden, a plant with grace,
A green guardian smiles, filling space.
With leaves like swords and a gentle touch,
Helping sunburns fade, isn't that much?

With a wink and a wiggle, it waits on the sill,
For the clumsy or careless, it's ready to thrill.
A friend for the heat, a pal for the cold,
Who knew that this plant could also be bold?

It rescues all scrapes, like a superhero,
With its slick, soothing gel, oh don't you know?
So when life gets messy and sticks like glue,
Nature's gentle arm will be there for you.

Wielding its magic, it takes quite the stand,
In a world full of chaos, it offers a hand.
With humor and charm, it battles the fray,
Who needs a fancy cream? Just give it a play!

Singing Succulents

Oh, the plants that sing in the bright sun's gaze,
In the pot with the dirt, they twirl and amaze.
They boast of their magic in each leafy song,
With whispers of giggles, it's never wrong.

They soak up the rays, but never complain,
Merry little wonders in sunshine or rain.
Like little green dancers, they sway to the beat,
A garden of laughter, such a vibrant treat.

With roots in the soil, and peps in their sway,
They're the jolliest bunch, come what may.
So let's all dance like these quirky ones do,
In a party of greens, we'll laugh like we grew!

Singing succulents, the jesters of green,
With humor as bright as the sunlight's sheen.
A twist of their leaves, and they chuckle with ease,
Creating a garden where worries just freeze!

Earth's Calm Companion

There's a friend in the dirt, who's calm as can be,
With a chill in its vibe, it's a plant, you see.
A soothing green presence, never in haste,
With a slurp of its essence, your fear's laid to waste.

It smiles through the chaos of life's little mess,
In a world full of noise, it brings you good rest.
A hug from the earth, it whispers, 'Just breathe,'
And all of your worries will quietly leave.

So if life's got you frazzled, come visit this mate,
With its gentle embrace, your troubles will abate.
It's rubbery charm and a wink just for fun,
This earthy companion is second to none.

So let's raise a glass to the friend that we share,
Under the sun, with incredible flair.
With a chuckle and grin, life's battles seem light,
Earth's calm companion, the joy of the night!

www.ingramcontent.com/pod-product-compliance
Lightning Source LLC
Chambersburg PA
CBHW070319120526
44590CB00017B/2735
9781805813156